Living With Sarcoidosis

DEFYING THE ODDS

MW00883936

OFFICIALLY WITHDRAWN

ADRIENNE ANDERSON

outskirtspress
DENVER, COLORADO

Outskirts Press, Inc.
http://www.outskirtspress.com

ISBN: 978-1-4787-1999-1

Outskirts Press and the "OP" logo are trademarks belonging to Outskirts Press, Inc.

PRINTED IN THE UNITED STATES OF AMERICA

This book is dedicated to all the wonderful people in my life who have been there with me and for me during my bouts with this disease. I also want to dedicate this book in loving memory of my sister, Necise. Thanks for the support! I LOVE YOU ALL!!!! ☺

Foreword

I wrote this book to inspire those of you who are struggling with sarcoidosis and to inform others up close and personal about the disease called sarcoidosis. No matter what type of disease you are suffering from, it is very important that you focus on healing. We all have choices in this life: you can either be miserable or you can be happy. I choose the latter. ☺ I refuse to let this disease get the best of me! ☺

I am so happy and grateful that GOD has blessed me with the mindset to keep on keeping on no matter what I go through. Meditate, stay prayed up, and believe that you are healed in the name of the Heavenly Father!

Peace, Blessings, and Love,
Adrienne

Table of Contents

Introduction

One of my biggest struggles in life is living with sarcoidosis. Sarcoidosis is a disease that can attack any organ in the body, and no one really knows what causes it. In some cases, it can be life threatening. I was diagnosed with sarcoidosis over 20 years ago. At that time not too many people knew about the disease, and I really had a hard time accepting it. There were times when I cried and became depressed. I hated how I looked while I was on Prednisone (steroids), and I even sheltered myself away from family and friends when I had a flare-up because I didn't want them to see me in a lot of pain. Basically, I tried to come to terms with why this happened to me.

I want to share my experiences with you so that you can get a better understanding about the disease and what we go through (from a patient's point of view).

Here's my story...........................

1

First Time I Heard of Sarcoidosis

It was the year 1990, and I was at home alone watching a weekly Sci-Fi television show. (It was about an Alien cop working alongside a Human cop solving crimes. The male aliens were the ones who bore the children.) In this particular episode, the alien was pregnant and about to deliver a baby. Suddenly I had a throbbing pain on the right side of my neck, and I felt a knot quickly growing under my skin. I said: "What the hell???" It literally FREAKED ME OUT because I was watching the show and all of a sudden this was happening to me! I COULDN'T BELIEVE IT! At first, I thought my mind was playing tricks on me, but I touched my neck; the pain was gone, but the knot was still there. I immediately called one of my friends to tell her what happened, but she didn't believe me. She laughed and said I was crazy telling her a story like that and that I shouldn't worry about it. As the old saying goes: "If it's not bothering you, don't bother it." I was very hesitant about seeing a doctor about it because I was afraid of hearing any bad news, so I left it alone.

A few weeks later, I was in a bad car accident, and I had to see an orthopedist for treatment. When he saw the knot on my neck, he said to me, "You might have sarcoidosis or lymphoma". I said, "What?" and he repeated it. (That was the first time I heard the name.) He didn't tell me about the disease; he just recommended that I make an appointment to see a physician.

Since I worked at a hospital, I made an appointment to see a physician there. My old boss referred me to one of his colleagues. The doctor worked in Research and wasn't seeing patients anymore, but as a favor agreed to see me in her office. She asked me why I was there, and I showed her the knot on my neck. She examined me and explained to me that she would try to see if she could drain fluid from the area. When she stuck the needle in and no fluid drained out, she told me that I would have to have a lymph node biopsy to determine what it was. She said that I had to be admitted into the hospital in order for the biopsy to be done. I was instructed to go for pre-admission testing to get medically cleared for the procedure as soon as possible.

A few days later, I was admitted to the hospital to have the biopsy done. Afterwards, the surgeon told me that three knots the size of golf balls were removed. He told me that the procedure went well, and it would be a couple of days before my results were known. Since the procedure was so extensive in my neck, I had to stay in the hospital for a few more days under observation.

Since I was an employee at the hospital, my co-workers regularly stopped by my room to check on me throughout the day. Whenever the nurses walked past my room, it was always filled with laughter. They said that there was no way I could be sick because I was having too much fun! ☺ A few days passed before I was discharged and able to return home.

The following week, I had an appointment with my doctor to get the results of my biopsy. She told me that the biopsy revealed that I had sarcoidosis. Since I didn't have a clue, I asked her what sarcoidosis was. She told me that it was a disease that could affect any organ in my body. She also said that no one knows what causes the disease, but if I ever ate red clay pies or played with porcupine cones, that was a possibility of how I got it. I started crying and said, "My family and I ate red clay pies because of its healing properties, and they didn't get it! Why me! I try to live right! I don't drink or do drugs! Maybe I should have been drinking or doing drugs!" She looked at me and said, "Then you would be dead." She tried to console me, and after I calmed down a little, she went on to explain the importance of having regular blood tests, keeping my doctor appointments, and paying close attention to any changes in my body. At that particular time, since I didn't have any symptoms, I didn't have to take any medication.

A short time later, I noticed that my eyes were becoming very sensitive to light, and they hurt whenever I drove at night. It always felt like everybody was driving with their high beams on. After suffering for a few days, I went back to the doctor, and told her about my eyes. She sent me to an ophthalmologist. After having my pupils dilated and being examined, the doctor said that I had sarcoidosis of the eyes. (If it goes untreated, glaucoma, cataracts, and blindness can occur.) She gave me some steroid drops to insert twice a day, and after a couple of weeks, my eyes were back to normal. She informed me that it is very important that I get an annual eye examination that includes getting my eyes dilated because some sarcoidosis-related eye problems do not have any symptoms.

A few months later, my doctor referred me to another physician because she had to devote all of her time to research. I am very grateful to GOD that I was blessed to have her in my life, especially during a time when most doctors knew very little about this disease. She taught me so much, and she explained everything in detail. She was so knowledgeable, and she helped me understand exactly what I needed to do to take good care of myself while living with this condition. She also taught me how to recognize the symptoms of a flare-up, so it was very difficult for other inexperienced doctors to BS around with me because I KNEW MY STUFF!!! ☺

2
My First Flare-Up

In 1991, I started experiencing shortness of breath. Whenever I inhaled, I felt excruciating pain under my left rib. The pain was so severe, all I could do was cry. I saw my doctor with my complaints, and she requested an x-ray and CT scan with dye. When the results came back, she told me that my spleen was inflamed, and that's what was causing the pain. She immediately prescribed 40 milligrams of Prednisone for me to take on a daily basis.

One morning as I got up out of bed, I noticed that my legs were numb, and I couldn't walk. I panicked! I called my boyfriend, and he came over right away. He did everything he could to help me. Since I had no feeling in my legs, he filled the bathtub with cold water. Then he picked me up and put me in the tub. He thought sitting in a tub of cold water for a few minutes would help bring feeling back into my legs, but it didn't work. My legs were still numb, so I called my doctor and told her what happened. When she told me that it was one of the side effects of the medication (a very rare one), I told her that I was going to stop taking it. She said I couldn't just stop taking it abruptly and that I would have to slowly be tapered off of it because I was on such a high dosage. She stressed the importance of taking the medication as prescribed because if I stopped taking it suddenly, my adrenal glands would shut down, and I would die. That scared the crap out of me, so I said, "GREAT!" Do you think I wanted to hear that? I was pissed! I told her that if I knew something like this was going to happen to me, I wouldn't have taken it! Well, she didn't take me off the medication because I needed it. Sometimes you have to weigh the benefits versus the risks, and in my case, the benefits outweighed the risks. So unfortunately, I had to wait for my breathing to improve before my dosage could be reduced. And that took a few months!!! But what could I do? Nothing at all.............

3

Double Pneumonia

In December, 1992, I developed a persistent cough that wouldn't go away. It had gotten so bad that I had to be taken to the emergency room by ambulance because I started experiencing shortness of breath and couldn't breathe. On arrival, I was immediately put on oxygen to help open up my lungs. After I was examined by the Emergency Room physician, he told me that I had to be admitted because I had double pneumonia. When he told me that I had to take Prednisone intravenously, I initially refused. (I didn't want to experience the same side effects from the medication that I experienced the previous year.) He got angry and said in a very stern voice, "You have to take it or you will die!" Well, that scared me enough to take it. Sadly for me it was New Year's Eve, and I was supposed to go to a party with my boyfriend.

After the doctor left the room, I called my boyfriend and told him what happened. He came to the hospital to visit me, and we laughed and told jokes to each other for hours. Before I knew it, visiting hours were over, and it was time for him to go. I tried to get him to stay with me in the hospital so that we could bring in the New Year together, but he was afraid to stay. The patient sharing the room with me was on a respirator, and he didn't want to be there in case she died that night. I just wanted him to hide in the closet until the security guard finished checking the rooms and then he could come out and spend the night with me. Unfortunately, he couldn't stay, so he left a little while later and went to our friends' New Year's Eve Party. As soon as the clock struck 12 midnight, I called my boyfriend and family and friends to wish them all a Happy New Year. It was exciting, but it wasn't the same. They were all partying and having a good time celebrating the New Year while I was cooped up in a hospital room on oxygen and Prednisone. There's nothing like being around a lot of people on such a joyous occasion! ☺

4

Second Hand Smoke and Sarcoidosis

Before I got sick, I used to be able to hang out with people who smoked cigarettes. I never had a problem with my family or friends smoking in my house or my car because it never bothered me. After I got sick, everything changed.

I remember going out one night with my friends to a birthday party. We were having a great time! I had just met a nice young man, and we danced and danced and danced! People were smoking, but I tried not to let it bother me. All of a sudden, I couldn't breathe, and I felt like I was about to pass out! The guy who was dancing with me noticed what was happening and immediately took me outside. I was literally gasping for air! I felt tightness in my chest, and I ended up going to the emergency room. The doctor asked me what happened. I told him that I had pulmonary sarcoidosis and that I inhaled cigarette smoke at the party. I was given oxygen and monitored for a few hours. He stressed the importance of letting my family and friends know that I couldn't be around cigarette smoke. I was sent home with instructions to stay away from events where smoking was allowed.

After that incident occurred, I told my family and friends that I couldn't be exposed to cigarette smoke anymore. I told them what happened at the birthday party, and how important it was for me to stay away from second hand smoke. When I told them that they could not smoke in my house or car anymore, they understood and didn't have a problem with it. Whenever they come to my house, they go outside to smoke, and they also smoke before they get into my car.

Although mostly everybody was okay with my decision, I had to cut off a few so-called friends because they wouldn't respect my wishes. I remember hanging out with some friends one night, and one of them got upset with me when I told her that she couldn't smoke in my car anymore. Do you know what that chick said to me? Well, she said, "You used to let me smoke in your car!" And I said, "Yeah! That was before I got sick! Now I cannot be around it!" (She knew I had pulmonary sarcoidosis.) You would think she'd be more understanding like the others, but she wasn't. I couldn't believe she was practically arguing with me about it. How inconsiderate of her to jeopardize my health! After that happened, that friendship was over! My health is the most important thing to me. I believe that if you don't care enough about me and my well-being, then you are not a true friend.

I often take a trip to South Carolina to visit my family. Whenever I'm there, I don't have to worry about compromising my health. They go into another room or smoke outside when I'm around. If one of my sisters has company at her place and they are smoking, she'll let me know, and I won't go inside or I'll go to another section of the house. Now that's love! It's funny though when we're outside. If they need to smoke, they stand far away from me so I don't have any contact. I'd have to let them know that they don't have to stand that far away because the smoke blows through the air. ☺ I'm happy they don't let my illness stop them from being around me. Whenever we get together, we have a BALL! Why should we let a little smoke come between us??? ☺

I heard that there were patients smoking marijuana for glaucoma, and I was curious to find out if it would work for patients with sarcoidosis. I was willing to try almost anything to avoid taking Prednisone again, so I spoke to a homeopathic doctor about it. He told me that there were patients who were smoking marijuana to improve their medical conditions, but he couldn't guarantee that it would work for me. I was willing to give it a shot, so I tried it. All it did was heighten my senses and get me sexually aroused. It didn't help my breathing, but I had fun that night!!! I did it for medicinal purposes only!!! ☺

When a man shows interest in me, one of the first things I ask is if he smokes or not. If he does, I let him know that I'm flattered, but I cannot go out with him because of my pulmonary disease. Believe it or not, they respect my honesty. It is very important to me that he doesn't smoke because I cannot get involved with a man who does. My health comes first. ☺

5

Sarcoidosis Support Group

I found out about a Sarcoidosis Symposium being held at a nearby medical facility, and I wanted to attend to get more information about the disease and to find out about joining a support group. I enjoyed listening to the lecturers, but I didn't enjoy the support session. Let me tell you: it was so depressing listening to people talk about their disease. I couldn't take it. The majority of the ones who got up to talk made my heart sad because they were miserable. All they did was complain, and no one had anything positive to say about their condition or how to cope with it. I had to get out of there because it was draining me mentally, emotionally, and physically. I'm sure there are support groups out there that are very encouraging and supportive, but this one group left a bad taste in my mouth, so I decided not to attend any more sessions.

At that point, I had made up my mind to be my own support system. I did whatever I had to do to build myself up: I prayed, performed daily meditation rituals, listened to motivational speakers and self empowerment CDs, interacted with family/friends, laughed a lot, and focused on being happy and making other people happy in the process. Whenever my friends found out that their family member/friend had sarcoidosis, they would ask me to talk to them. They loved the fact that no matter what I was going through, I stayed in positive spirits and focused on healing. I would help them understand what the disease was. I remembered everything my first doctor explained to me about sarcoidosis, and I shared that information with them. Many didn't understand and were afraid, but I would help ease their pain and frustration or confusion and let them know that they could still live a happy, productive life after being diagnosed with sarcoidosis.

There were a few negative people I tried to talk to when I heard they had sarcoidosis, but no matter what I said, they continued to talk in a pessimistic way. I tried to get them to meditate and to start radiating positive energy, but they didn't want to hear it. They didn't think it would work. They wanted me to join their pity party, and I wasn't doing it. Since they weren't receptive to what I was saying, I politely parted ways and continued to focus on me. ☺

I enjoy and always make time to talk to people about sarcoidosis. I get a great sense of satisfaction when I am able to help someone understand and cope with their condition (living with this disease). I also help family members and friends understand what their family member or friend is going through and how they can help.

Sarcoidosis affects people all over the world: Scandinavian, German, Irish, and Puerto Rican, as well as African American and people of Caribbean descent. No one knows why, but it has occurred often enough in the United States for Congress to have declared a National Sarcoidosis Awareness Day in 1990.

Sarcoidosis affects both male and female of all races and ages. It is most commonly found in people between the ages of 20 and 40, and it rarely occurs in children. Although Caucasian women and men can get sarcoidosis, it occurs more frequently among African American people. African American women get sarcoidosis two times as often as African American men. As of today in the United States, it is estimated that about 11 in 100,000 Caucasian Americans have sarcoidosis, and about 36 in 100,000 African Americans have sarcoidosis. The percentage of people with sarcoidosis is higher, but because the disease has been misdiagnosed and mistaken for other diseases, the true estimates are unknown.

Most people with sarcoidosis can live normal, active lives. It is not common, but in a certain percentage of situations, sarcoidosis can be fatal. The outcome of sarcoidosis depends upon the severity of the illness.

6

Negative Energy

After I got sick, I had to separate myself from negative people because they weren't healthy for me. I've always been a very positive person, and I like being around positive people. If I'm trying to help you, and you're constantly being negative, I can't deal with you because: 1) It mentally drains me; and 2) It causes a lot of stress on my body. Stress is the #1 contributing factor of sarcoidosis, and I cannot afford to get stressed out or sick! What I really enjoy is spreading my positive energy around and giving love and hugs to everyone. ☺

I had a friend who was a pessimist in the worse way. She was always complaining about something. She never had anything positive to say about anyone or anything; she was just negative, negative, negative. One day, while we were hanging out getting something to eat, a young lady stepped out of a nice, new Mercedes convertible. Instead of her saying that the lady was driving a nice car, she said, "She thinks she's all that because she's driving that car!" I couldn't believe she said that! I just looked at her, shaking my head, and said, "Girl, you shouldn't say that. When you're jealous of another person's blessings, you block your own blessings. What you should have said was she was driving a nice car, and one day, you will too." That's how I think. But there was always something going on with her. Her negative energy took a toll on my body. She was making it more and more difficult to deal with her, and I couldn't take it anymore. After a while, it had gotten to the point where whenever she called and started talking negative, I'd get a sharp pain in my chest. That's when I knew my friendship with her had come to an end.

I also had a co-worker who used to come into my office on a daily basis complaining about what was happening in her department. Before she came into my office, I'd be happy and filled with energy, and after she left, I was mentally and emotionally exhausted! One day, I had to say to her, "I don't mind you coming to my office to vent, but you have to decide what you're going to do. You have two choices: you can either deal with it or do something about it." I also told her that whenever she came to my office complaining about the same thing every day and not doing anything about it, it was wearing me out. I explained to her how her negative energy was affecting me, and it wasn't healthy. She said, "Well, I won't come to your office then." I said, "Okay. Take care, and have a good day." She left my office upset, and she didn't stop by for three months. When she finally did stop by again, her attitude was totally different, and everything she spoke about was positive. ☺

Being positive brings about more positive. I try to look at all situations from a positive point of view no matter how bad the situation may be. Whenever someone talks to me, and they're projecting negative energy, I try to change the conversation to a more positive one. If they continue to dwell on the negative issue, I end the conversation very quickly. People don't understand the impact negative energy has on the body. That's one of the causes why people get sick! I've realized that when I deal with people who are always negative about everything, it affects me internally, and I get sick. I don't want to be sick. Do you???

7

Another Flare-Up

In 1993, I started working at another hospital facility. A few months later, I started having shortness of breath again. No matter what I did, I had to take a break before going any further. I couldn't walk up a flight of stairs, walk short distances, dance, or do anything that caused any exertion because I could barely breathe. I knew something was wrong, so I went into my boss's office to tell him what was going on. He was really concerned about me, so he referred me to a pulmonary specialist. She requested a series of tests: chest x-ray, CT scan with/without the dye, and a blood gas (test where blood is drawn from the artery in the wrist to determine the oxygen level in the blood – very painful). After the results came back, she told me that I had a flare-up and had to take Prednisone. She prescribed 60 milligrams of Prednisone daily! I had only taken the medication for two weeks and gained 20 pounds! When I called and told her, she didn't believe me, so I went to her office so she could see for herself. She immediately tapered me down to 40 milligrams, but I had to take Prednisone for eight months. What a bummer! I was miserable!

It had gotten to the point that I couldn't work a full eight hours. I could barely do anything without gasping for air. I could barely walk because of the severe back pain due to the recent weight gain. My boss was very understanding about my medical condition and allowed me to work four hours a day instead of eight. Every day I would go to work from 8:00am to 12:00pm, and then I'd go home and rest.

After my condition improved and I was able to work full-time again, I went into my boss's office to talk to him and to thank him for being so understanding. He said to me in a direct tone: "The reason you still have your job is because you do more work in half a day than most people do in a full day. That's why I kept you on. Any other person would have been fired." I was glad to hear him say that, and that's why he approved of me working part-time until I was better. He never gave me any indication that I had anything to worry about. I was very thankful and appreciative that he was pleased enough with my work performance to allow me to keep working. ☺

8

Other Symptoms

It was very difficult for me to accept the fact that I'd always have to take Prednisone whenever I had a flare-up. Prednisone is the most common drug prescribed to treat patients with sarcoidosis.

With each episode, I suffered with more problems besides shortness of breath and an inflamed spleen. I had severe joint pain in my fingers, a persistent cough, and I was always dead tired! I'm a very light sleeper, but whenever I'd have a flare-up, I'd sleep through anything.

I'll never forget the time when I dozed off with a pot on the stove. I woke up coughing in a smoke-filled house, and firemen were banging on my door! I didn't hear the smoke detector, and I didn't smell anything until it was almost too late! If the firemen hadn't gotten to my house when they did, I probably wouldn't be here to tell my story. Thank GOD it was a glass pot!

9

Alternative Treatment

A few months had passed, and I had another flare-up. I knew I was sick, and I needed to do something about it. I didn't want to take Prednisone anymore because the side effects were unbearable sometimes. I decided to try something different, so I looked into an alternative form of health care. I went to a homeopathic doctor for treatment. I spent hundreds of dollars hoping his natural methods would help my condition, but it didn't, so I had to break down and make an appointment to see my pulmonary specialist.

I went to my doctor a few weeks later, and I told her that I had gone to see a homeopathic doctor for treatment to see if I'd get positive results. She said that she understood my reluctance to take Prednisone, but she informed me of the dangers involved in delaying medical treatment when it's needed. She sent me to Radiology to get a chest x-ray. When she reviewed the film, she explained how not seeking treatment for my disease when I had a flare-up caused permanent scar tissue damage on my lungs. Now, whenever I get a chest x-ray, I am constantly asked if I have emphysema or if I've been exposed to anyone with emphysema. I always tell them, "No. I have pulmonary sarcoidosis."

10

Weight Gain and Cravings

I gained so much weight while taking Prednisone! I ate everything in sight, and whatever I craved, I had to have! I'll never forget the time when I had a craving for a coconut custard pie in May, 1994, and it had to be a particular brand. I checked several stores for it. My aunt even went to several stores to try and find it for me. Since we didn't have any luck, we went directly to a well-known bakery and asked for it. They said that coconut custard pie was a special pie that wasn't made during the summer. When I heard that, I started to cry! I felt like a drug addict! I had to have that pie! To ease my misery, we drove to another bakery and bought another brand of coconut custard pie, but it tasted like garbage! My aunt felt so bad for me that she looked up the recipe, bought the ingredients, and baked me a coconut custard pie to help soothe my pain. Now, my aunt is a good baker, and she always bakes delicious cakes and pies, but it didn't work! I told her that I was grateful for what she did, but it didn't taste like the pie I wanted. I went through withdrawal symptoms like a person on drugs, and I had to accept the fact that I wouldn't be getting any coconut custard pie anytime soon.......

A few months later, my condition got better, and I was taken off the medication. My aunt had gone grocery shopping and came across the coconut custard pies. She was so excited that she grabbed two pies and couldn't wait to get them to me. When she told me that she had bought them, I looked at her and said, "Why? I don't eat that kind of pie!" She looked at me like I was crazy! I only had a craving for that pie while I was on the Prednisone! I told her that I didn't mean it in a nasty way; I just didn't eat it. She understood. Good thing she also liked them! ☺

I had another episode where I got upset when I didn't get what I wanted while taking Prednisone. My best friend was going to the store across the street from our job and asked me if I wanted anything. I told her that I wanted a Payday candy bar. When she returned, she said they didn't have any Paydays, so she got me a Snickers. I looked at her like she was crazy and said, "I didn't ask for a damn Snickers! I told you to get me a Payday!" I scared my poor friend almost to death. She never saw me like this before. She said that she was going to try another store to find me one, but I told her to forget it. I felt so bad afterwards for snapping at her, and I apologized about it. The beauty of it was she, like my aunt, knew that it wasn't me talking and acting like a crazy person. They knew it was the medication making me act like a lunatic! My friend, however, mentioned that I should stop expecting people to automatically understand what I'm going through because they aren't aware of the affect the medication has on me. I'm telling you: I had it bad!!!

Anytime I tasted something and really enjoyed it while I was on Prednisone, I had to eat it every day until I stopped taking the medication. I had no control over it! It was the cravings!!! If I ate a candy bar, I had to have another one and another one and another one! I ate so many candy bars that my best friend starting eating them too, and she didn't like candy bars, you go figure! ☺

I'll never forget this: In 2005, I went to McDonald's for a Big Mac, biggie fries, and a caramel sundae because I was hungry. BIG MISTAKE! After that, I had to go to McDonald's every day to get that same meal. I admit it; I was addicted!

People don't really understand what a person's body is going through when we are taking Prednisone. Sometimes you get uncontrollable cravings and have to eat what you crave. I'll never forget what a co-worker said to me when I said I had a craving for a Snickers bar. She said to me, "You don't need to eat that. What you should be eating is carrots and celery sticks." I looked at her and said, "I have to have that candy bar, and I have no control over it." She then said to me that I did have control over what I ate and that I was using Prednisone as an excuse to eat what I want to eat. That's when I got pissed off! I asked her if she had ever been on Prednisone. When she said no, I said to her, "Okay then. Don't tell me how my body should react while I'm taking this medicine. One of the side effects is increased appetite and strong cravings for food. So until you experience what I'm going through, keep your comments to yourself!" Then I walked away. Do people really believe that we purposely want to eat foods that will blow us up? Come on now. Wake up and smell the coffee. If you know a person before he/she starts taking Prednisone, you would notice the change in their eating habits.

A few years later, the same co-worker had a terrible accident and had to take Prednisone for a long period of time. When she returned to work about 30 to 40 pounds heavier, she came to me with an apology. She said that she really couldn't understand or accept what I was going through until she experienced it for herself. She felt bad for saying what she said to me, but I told her it was okay. Now she knows firsthand!

In 2009, I was in a different frame of mind based on my past experiences with Prednisone and food cravings. I decided to make better food choices while I was on Prednisone; I ate home-cooked meals, and I stayed away from fast food. The only thing I craved every day was turkey bacon and scrambled eggs on a toasted everything bagel with mayo. I had it one day at my aunt's house, and I was hooked until I got off the medication. Of course, my cholesterol went through the roof, but I changed my diet and my cholesterol levels went back to normal very quickly. I wasn't trying to get on cholesterol medication too. ☺

11

The Effects of Prednisone On My Body

My body also undergoes extreme physical changes when I'm on Prednisone. I go through a complete transformation! One day I look normal, and then the following week, I look deformed with a moon pie face, and my body swells up like a balloon. Sometimes my temples hurt because of the swelling, and I cannot wear my eyeglasses after a while because they become too tight on my face. I REALLY HATE THE WAY I LOOK WHILE I'M TAKING PREDNISONE! One day I was walking down the street feeling good about myself, and a guy yelled out, "Damn girl, you look good! Keep lifting those weights!" I got upset because I wasn't lifting any weights!

No matter how I looked, my family and friends constantly reminded me of the beautiful person I was within. They said that I had beautiful skin, I had a beautiful smile, and I would quickly lose the weight once I got off the medicine. I appreciated the compliments, but it didn't make me feel better because I had to constantly look at myself in the mirror.

I also have to deal with the reactions I get from people when I have another flare-up. Time and time again, I tell them that my sarcoidosis is acting up again, and I'm back on the medicine. Some people can't help themselves; they are just IGNORANT!!! A former co-worker saw me while I was sick, and said very loudly, "Damn girl! What are you eating?" She knew I had sarcoidosis and that I had another flare-up. I said angrily back to her, "What the hell do you mean what am I eating? You know I'm on that damn Prednisone!" She really pissed me off! I already have a complex about my weight, and was trying to deal with how I looked while on Prednisone. Do you actually think I want to hear something like that???

Physical appearances aren't the only side effects of the drug. My body also gets depleted of Potassium. When I don't have enough Potassium in my system, I suffer with severe cramping in my legs and feet.

One day, I went to visit my best friend. (She was eight months pregnant at the time.) We were laughing and talking, and then all of a sudden, I got a cramp in my right big toe. I jumped up and tried to walk it out, but it was traveling up my leg too quickly. I punched, slapped, and massaged my leg, but nothing worked. I started walking back and forth from the front of her house to the back of her house trying to get some relief. Shortly after that, I got a cramp in the other leg, and that's when I knew I was in trouble! The cramp traveled from the back of my leg down to my feet. She saw the anguish on my face, and asked me what was wrong. I took off my shoe, and we both watched in amazement as my big toe stretched to the right while my other toes curled up into a tight ball. She said, "OH MY GOD! WHAT SHOULD I DO?" And that's when I told her that I needed some Potassium. She rushed into the kitchen to get a banana. She usually keeps bananas in the house, but today of all days, she didn't have any! I was almost in tears! She saw how much pain I was in, so she rushed to her truck and drove to the store to get me some Potassium (thank GOD it was a short distance away). I felt bad knowing that she had to drive, but I couldn't do it, and she was very insistent on going. When she returned, I was still pacing the floor to no avail. Once I popped a Potassium tablet in my mouth, 5 minutes later, the cramps were gone! She was my savior!!! I LOVE YOU GIRL!!! ☺

12

Weight Gain and Severe Back Pain

After my first flare-up, it seemed like every few months (for the next 13 years) I had to get back on the medication for my breathing. I'd have a break for a few months, and then I'd get sick all over again. And every time I got on the medication, I gained a whole lot of weight. It was a really bad situation for me. I would complain about having to take the medication, and everybody always said the same thing, "Why are you worried about gaining weight? You have a pretty face, and a beautiful smile." And I'd say to them that I wasn't worried about the weight gain; I worried about the severe back pain I suffered with due to the weight gain. I have three herniated discs in my lower back from a previous car accident, and whenever I gained a lot of weight, I was always in excruciating pain. I couldn't stand long, sit long, walk short distances or anything without suffering. It was kind of depressing for me. There were times when I had to literally sit in the middle of the floor wherever I was just to relieve the pain in my lower back. It wasn't that I didn't care. I just needed some relief!

One day, my best friend and I were in Macy's when my back started aching. I had to sit in the middle of the floor where people were shopping. The pain was so bad that it didn't matter where I was sitting. I just needed some relief!!! My friend didn't understand the pain I was in. At first, she was embarrassed because people kept looking at me.

Then she realized that I must really be in a lot of pain to put myself in such a humiliating position. She felt so bad for me, but she tried not to show it. It wasn't until she experienced severe back pain that she could truly understand what I was going through. I wouldn't wish that pain on anyone.

I'll never forget the time when I decided not to bother anybody and took a chance and walked to the grocery store. I barely made it there, but on the way back, I was in trouble! I was one block from my house, and I couldn't make it. I hurt so bad that I was ready to lie on the sidewalk. A man who was driving by saw how much pain I was in and asked me if I was alright. I told him I was in excruciating pain! He told me that he lived on the block, and he would give me a ride home. Honey, I got in the car! He could have been a serial killer, a rapist, or even the Devil himself, but I got into that car. I was in too much pain to turn it down. He was kind enough to drop me off. I got his address, and sent him a thank you card to show my appreciation for what he had done. GOD BLESS HIM!!! ☺

The joke is that I'm always on a yo-yo diet. Every time I take Prednisone, I gain a lot weight, and as soon as I get off of it, I focus on losing it. It has been a huge struggle for me fighting the battle of the bulge, but at least I know how to do it. ☺

13

Insomnia

One of the side effects of taking Prednisone is insomnia. I have had many sleepless nights because of it. I'd be up late at night reading or talking to a friend until the wee hours of the morning because I couldn't sleep. I'd go to work and do my job, but there were times when I was almost comatose. I remember driving home from work in bumper-to-bumper traffic and falling asleep behind the wheel. My car bumped the car in front of me, and when that happened, I woke up. The guy and I got out of our cars, and I apologized to him for bumping his car. I told him that I had dozed off, and he said that I'd better be careful going home and to get some sleep. Luckily for me, there wasn't any damage; I just lightly bumped it, THANK GOD! I had to get some much needed sleep, so my aunt suggested that I drink warm milk at night before going to bed. It helped a little; I was able to get a little rest, but I need my proper sleep. I tried Valerian tea which is supposed to be good for helping you relax and go to sleep. It didn't help me, so I stopped drinking it.

My aunt also told me to place lavender oil on my night stand and to rub it under my nose. She said that it is known for helping people relax and go to sleep. It did relax me, but I didn't go to sleep. I do love the way it smells though! ☺

Every once in a while, I take over the counter sleep-aids and prescribed sleeping pills. I don't take them often because I don't like feeling groggy the next day. I only take them on an as needed basis. ☺

14

New Doctor – New Plan

I had another flare-up in 2004, and since my pulmonary doctor relocated to another state, my medical doctor referred me to another pulmonary specialist. He did the same series of tests as done previously, and the end result was that I had to get back on Prednisone. He followed me for awhile; the only problem I had with him was that he didn't take me and treating my disease as seriously as I had hoped. When he would see me and I'd be in great spirits, I got the impression that he didn't think that I was really sick, and therefore, I didn't initially get the proper attention that I needed to treat me for my disease. I had to stress to him how I was feeling before he would actually do something about it. Of course, he'd put me on Prednisone, but as far as getting **thorough** follow-ups, he didn't do it. I had to wait 2 sometimes 3 hours to see him, and then he would only see me for 5 minutes (if that long). I had to literally tell him that he needed to do his job better because I was really sick and getting really frustrated. I was prepared to find another physician. I knew then that I had to change my mindset and focus on beating this disease because I didn't want to rely on doctors who weren't really concerned about my well-being. I can't help that I'm a very positive, uplifting person no matter how I feel! Should I walk around looking depressed, miserable, and in a lot of pain to get adequate treatment? What's up with that???

Eventually, I was tapered off the medication, and then I focused on getting the weight off to help relieve my back pain. I also decided that if I got sick again, I would be seen by doctors where I worked from now on because I had a great relationship with them, and I knew they would take good care of me.

15

Chest Pain

In June, 2005, I was working in my office, and suddenly, I felt like I was going to pass out. I was experiencing some chest pain, and I was sweating profusely. My old boss just happened to stop by my office, and when she looked at me, she had a look of alarm on her face. She asked me what was wrong, and I told her that I was having some chest pain and felt like I was going to pass out. I told her that I was just going to go home and lie down because I was tired. She said to me, "No you're not! I'm walking you down to the emergency room because you don't look good. You're sweating, your hands are damp, and you look like you could pass out at any moment." She then proceeded to take me to the emergency room where they put me on a stretcher and hooked me up to a heart monitor. As usual, because I'm a sarcoidosis patient, I was admitted as a precautionary measure, and extensive tests were done to make sure I didn't have sarcoidosis of the heart. All my tests came back okay, and I was discharged a few days later.

16

Dizziness

In May, 2007, I was admitted into the hospital because I was experiencing dizziness and loss of balance, and my heart was beating fast. The room was spinning, and whenever I got up to walk, I had to hold on to something to keep from falling. I would only take a few steps, and my heart would start beating rapidly. I was examined by a doctor, in particular, who left a bad taste in my mouth. He didn't feel that anything was wrong with me. He requested a couple of tests, and because they came back okay, he was ready to discharge me. I told him that I was still experiencing dizziness and that my balance was off, but he was insistent on getting me out of the hospital as soon as possible. He said that I looked okay, and I tried to explain to him that I was okay as long as I was sitting down; everything would happen after I got up to walk. I even told him to have one of the residents walk with me to see what would happen, but he didn't seem too concerned about it. And to top it off, when he found out that I was an employee of the hospital, he had the audacity to say to me in front of the residents, "You're not really sick. You just don't want to work." I looked at him pissed off, and said, "First of all, you don't know me. I'm one of the hardest working people at this hospital. You can ask anybody!" And he said, "If you are that great, why weren't you selected as employee of the month?" I was livid! I couldn't believe he said that to me! I told him that he needed to do his job and focus on what was wrong with me and why I was having these symptoms instead of who was employee of the month. He had a whole lot of nerve talking to me like that! I even said to him, "You know I have sarcoidosis! Why don't you request a Neurology consultation?" And he said, "All they want to do is run a lot of tests. I'm not doing it." He said that they would monitor me for one more day, and then discharge me. I said to him, "If you discharge me, and something happens to me, you're going to have a problem." Of course, the following day, he discharged me, and right after I had gone downstairs, I started feeling the same way again and had to go back on the unit. When the resident who had just discharged me saw me again, he asked what had happened. I told him that I still had the same problem. I was readmitted, and since the doctor never requested a Neurology consultation, I called and requested one myself. (I know everybody at the hospital. ☺) The neurologist came to my room, examined me, and did some tests. The following day, I had to deal with that same nasty doctor again. He walked into my room, and said that he was discharging me again. By then, I was really fed up with his attitude and how I was being treated, so I told him not to talk to me anymore. I told him that he was rude, obnoxious, and very disrespectful, and I refuse to have anyone talk to me in this manner. I also said to him that he was very unprofessional, and I was getting a second opinion from another doctor. He stood there and told the residents that I had that right. I got on the phone, called my Associate Director who knew I was pissed off, and he in turn, told me to call the Director of Medicine. I called the Director and explained what had happened to me, what the doctor said to me in front of the residents, and how he treated me. He was very apologetic, and said that he would send one of his colleagues to examine me.

A few hours later, another doctor came to examine me. She asked me what was wrong, and I told her about my symptoms. I explained to her that everything was fine while I was sitting, but as soon as I got up to walk around, the symptoms would reappear. I knew the only way she would understand is if she accompanied me down the hall.

Before we left my room, she took my pressure and checked my pulse. Then we went for a walk. After I took a few steps out of my room, all of a sudden, I felt faint, my pulse started racing, and I was dizzy. She immediately took my pulse and was surprised at how fast it was beating because I had only taken a few steps. She also noticed that I looked pale. That's when I said, "I told you it would happen after I got up." She helped walk me back to my room, and said that she would follow-up with me. She also said that she would talk to the Director about it as well.

The following day, the Director of Medicine, came by to visit. He was very apologetic about not being able to see me sooner, and I told him I understood that he was a very busy man. I told him that I really appreciated him taking time out of his busy schedule to see me, and also for allowing his colleague to examine me. She was excellent! She was very thorough, and she knew that my complaints were valid because she observed for herself the drastic change in my vital signs when I exerted myself. All the necessary tests were performed, and they all came back okay. I could not be discharged until I felt better, so I had to stay another day. I was determined to get out of there because I wanted to go to my sister's wedding. I had a flight to catch that Friday night (5/4/07 – she was getting married the following day), so I asked one of my friends to bring me some Gatorade. I figured something had to work! I drank a couple of bottles of it that night, and one that morning. After breakfast, I got up and tried to walk. I walked slowly down the hall of the unit. Since I was able to walk a little more without any symptoms, I did it a few times that day.

The next day, I drank some more Gatorade and got up to walk again. Guess what? I actually walked slowly around the whole unit. I felt a little dizzy, but I was much better. ☺ I saw the Director on the floor, and I was so excited sharing my good news about walking the whole unit. I told him that I felt much better and wanted to know if I could be discharged because I wanted to catch my flight to South Carolina to go to my sister's wedding. He said that I could be discharged as long as I continued to feel better throughout the day. Later on that day, I was discharged, and I went straight to the airport! I didn't even have time to go home and get my luggage. It was the first time I felt free flying without anything! I had to go shopping early the following day before the wedding took place, and I was so happy I made it. It was a beautiful ceremony, and my sister was a beautiful bride. ☺ She told me she would have understood if I didn't make it, but I knew I had to be there! I still felt a little dizzy, so I just took it easy the rest of the weekend. By the time I got back home, I was 100% better, PRAISE GOD!!! ☺

17

Changing Professions

For many years, I worked in the Department of Obstetrics and Gynecology, and I LOVED MY JOB! Although I worked in a very stress-filled position, I really enjoyed what I did. I had a great relationship with my co-workers and other employees at the hospital. I also had an open door policy, so everybody knew they could come to my office anytime for any reason, and I would be there for them. I was MOTHER LOVE! ☺

Eventually, my job started taking a toll on me, and I started having chest pain on a regular basis. I was already complaining of headaches, so one day, my aunt said to me, "That job is going to kill you. You need to pray about it, and give it to GOD." I thought about what she said, and I prayed to GOD for guidance. The Lord spoke to me in my dream and said to leave my job, and do something I love. The next morning, I woke up at 6:00am and wrote my boss a letter of resignation. After I wrote that letter, it felt like a burden was lifted off my shoulders. I went to work and told everybody that I had given my boss two weeks notice. They were in SHOCK! They asked me why, and I told them that I was starting to get sick and had to do what was best for me. I tried to tell them that the stress was killing me, and I had to leave while I was still able to walk out of there. I said to them that it would be better to see me when I came back to visit as opposed to seeing me leave in a pine box. I also told them that I was starting my own travel business, and since I love to travel, why not do something I love? I got mixed responses. The majority of them were happy for me; then there were some people who tried to convince me not to leave saying the economy was bad and nobody was traveling. I told them that everybody needs to get a break sometimes, and people will take a vacation. I didn't allow anyone to discourage me from doing what I wanted to do.

Two weeks later, I left the hospital, and started doing my own thing. I was very happy with the decision I made, and I felt great! I also believed by faith that I wouldn't get sick again, so I gave away all my big clothes. I didn't keep one stitch because I constantly affirmed to myself that I was well and that I wouldn't have another recurrence. **BIG MISTAKE**!!! I should have at least kept a few pieces and tucked them away in the back of my closet because in December, 2008, I started getting sick again.......

18

Neurosarcoidosis

In December, 2008, I went to the emergency room complaining of severe headaches. When the doctor asked me how long I had been getting the headaches, I told him that I had been suffering with them on a daily basis since 2007 and was taking Tylenol and Motrin to try and ease the pain. He asked me if I had any nausea or vomiting, and I told him that for the past week, I had been throwing up everything I ate. After my examination, the Emergency Room physician recommended that I see the neurologist. A neurologist was not on call at the hospital that weekend, so he gave me a Neurology consult form and told me to make an appointment to see a neurologist as soon as possible.

The following week I had an appointment to see a neurologist. He asked me the reason for my visit, and I told him about my history of headaches since 2007. He did several tests, and when those tests came back negative, he requested an MRI with/without the dye. A few days later, I went to his office to get my results. He proceeded to tell me that I had swelling on the brain, and it was neurosarcoidosis. At first, it didn't hit me. The next thing I said to him was, "Okay, so when do we start treatment?" He told me that he really didn't treat patients who had neurosarcoidosis and that I had to find another neurologist who specialized in treating patients with the disease. After he walked out of his office, it suddenly hit me, and I started crying profusely. A few minutes later, he came back into his office and gave me a copy of the report. I thanked him for his services, and walked to my car feeling really sad. I then called my auntie, my family, and friends to tell them the news...............

The following day, I went to the hospital where I used to work to talk to the head neurologist and pulmonary specialist. I told them about my MRI results and that I was diagnosed with neurosarcoidosis. Since I knew they were both excellent doctors and I trusted their medical expertise, I asked them if they would provide me with the medical care I needed. They both agreed to take care of me. I gave them a copy of my MRI report, and they started requesting all kinds of tests: blood work, chest x-ray, CT scan, nuclear scan, another MRI, etc. Then the treatment began. Both doctors agreed to put me on 40 milligrams of Prednisone daily and have follow up appointments with them once a month.

I suffered terribly at night. I already had headaches during the day, but at night, they were worse! My head felt like it was going to explode! The headaches weren't regular headaches either. They were sharp, stabbing pains on the top right side of my head that radiated to the back of my head and down to my neck. All I could do was lie in a cradle position and cry and try to rock myself to sleep. There was nothing I could do to relieve myself of that pain. I wouldn't wish that on my worse enemy! Many times, I suffered alone at home because I didn't want anyone to see what I was really going through. I still laughed and talked to everybody on the phone, and that definitely made a difference. No matter how much pain I was in, I still continued to smile and be in happy spirits because I knew that what I was going through was temporary and that soon I would be back to my happy-go-lucky healthy self.

I remember one time feeling depressed, and I needed to talk to somebody. It was about 8:00pm. I called my aunt, and she could hear it in my voice. For a long time, I led people to believe that I was okay with my medical condition and that I wasn't troubled by what I was going through, but that night, I couldn't take it anymore. I broke down and cried hysterically! I was just TIRED!!! I was tired of being sick, tired of being in pain, tired of not getting any sleep at night, just tired of being tired! I was just tired of going through what I was going through! I was almost ready to give up! My aunt was so patient and understanding. She talked to me for a long time, and after I got off the phone, I felt much better. I also called to talk to my best friend. We laughed and talked for a while too. I was depressed for a minute, but after my phone conversations with my lifesavers, I was back on track. I was back to thinking happy thoughts and being the happy, positive person that I was. I had to remember that there are people out there whose conditions are 10 times worst than mine. THANK YOU LADIES! I LOVE YOU!!! ☺

Whenever I went to the hospital for my doctor appointments, my friends couldn't believe how positive and upbeat I was despite how much pain I was in. I always told them that I'd be fine; this was just a bump in the road, and I refused to let this disease keep me down. I'd be joking around knowing my head was pounding, but I was still happy. I continued to spread joy not only for them, but for me.

They call me Mother Love at the hospital because no one can walk past me without getting some love. I hug and kiss everybody. I have to go to the hospital two hours before my appointment because I know everybody and have to give them love. As soon as I walk through the door, people's faces light up, and they rush to me and give me a hug. I always show love to everyone there, and it is reciprocated. One day, a friend of mine saw me waiting to see the neurologist, and he got a little teary-eyed because he didn't know I was sick. He said that it hurt him to see such a beautiful person as myself suffering like I was; he said that he could think of a couple of people who he'd like to see suffer like that. I laughed and told him that I was in good hands, and that everything would be alright. ☺

19

Topamax

My neurologist knew how much I suffered with severe lower back pain when I gained a lot of weight, so she put me on a medication called Topamax (usually given to patients who have seizures). One of the benefits of taking it is that it slows down the weight gaining process. I was excited about taking it because I didn't want to gain a lot of weight and suffer while taking Prednisone like I had done in the past. What she didn't tell me was that one of the side effects of taking this drug was short term memory loss. I couldn't understand why I was forgetting things, and it was becoming more and more difficult for me to express myself! I'd be talking to my best friend about something and couldn't verbalize what I was trying to say. I couldn't get the words out, and simple things that used to come so easy to me were hard to remember. One day, I was talking to my best friend, and I was trying to tell her to pass me something on her desk, but I couldn't say what it was; I kept saying to pass me the thing. And she kept saying, "What thing?" And I kept saying, "The thing!" I was referring to a pen, but at the time, I couldn't say it. When she laughed and asked what was wrong with me, I started crying. I told her that it wasn't funny; I can't remember! Then I told her how I was forgetting a lot of things. At that point, she started crying too because she didn't realize the effect the medication was having on me. I asked her why she was crying. She said that she was crying because I was crying and that she felt so bad for me. She was very apologetic about the whole situation, and I told her it was okay. I knew she loved me, and wouldn't make fun of me on purpose. ☺

The icing on the cake was when I couldn't remember The Lord's Prayer. I said that prayer a million times in my life, so can you imagine how upsetting it was for me to start praying and stop mid-sentence because I couldn't remember the words??? I started crying again! I didn't understand what was going on! I thought I was losing my mind! The whole day I tried to recite it to see if it would come back to me, and it didn't. When I told my neurologist about it, she told me that short-term memory loss was one of the side effects of the drug. I told her that I had to get off that medication because I didn't like the way I felt. (I had to be tapered off that medication as well.) She sent me to a neuro-psychologist for testing, and I cried there too because I couldn't remember the names of simple things that I knew. My neurologist told me not to worry too much. She said that my memory would come back, but maybe not all of it.

I'm back to normal now, and I'm still smart as a whip! ☺ I won't know if I don't remember something until a situation presents itself. My uncle tried to help me remember something that happened a few years ago, but my mind drew a blank. Still does............. Now I look at it as just having a senior moment, and I keep it moving! ☺

20

Socializing

After I started taking Prednisone for neurosarcoidosis, I stopped socializing and traveling for a while. The excessive weight gain and severe lower back pain caused me to refrain from many of the activities that I used to enjoy. I didn't hang out with my family and friends because I was in so much pain when I had to get up and walk. Even the walk from my bedroom to the bathroom was almost unbearable! I literally felt like crawling; that's how much pain I was in.

My aunt bought me a stool to carry with me when I traveled because I couldn't stand for long periods of time. I took that stool with me everywhere I went. If I had to go to the doctor, grocery store, or wherever, I would walk a few steps, and then stop and sit on my stool. When I was ready to walk again, I did the same thing. It took me forever to get from point A to point B, but I did it. It was very depressing. With that being said, I chose to do nothing but go to the doctor and stay at home. Since it just hurt too much to try to walk or do anything, my bed became my new best friend.

One day, I went to my chiropractor's office for a treatment. She asked me how I was doing, and then all of a sudden, tears just started coming down. I couldn't stop crying. She knew how my life used to be, so she understood my pain. She said that I didn't look like my happy self, and she sensed that something was wrong. I broke down and talked to her about how I was feeling. Here I was a person who was always on the go, visiting family and friends, hanging out, traveling, just doing things, and now I couldn't do anything. I was miserable! I told her that the only thing I did was lie in my bed, and she advised me to get out of that bed and to start sitting in the living room. She said that staying in bed wasn't healthy; I would end up depressed. She talked to me for a long time, and afterwards, I left her office in better spirits. I thank GOD for blessing me to have that conversation with her. The next time she saw me, I was happy and smiling and singing I'VE GOT A NEW ATTITUDE!!! ☺

I had already paid to go on a cruise with my family in April, 2009, so I decided to take the trip. That was the worst trip of my life! I was in good spirits; my body was just JACKED UP!!! I couldn't really enjoy myself nor could I show them a good time because I was still taking Prednisone, still gaining weight, and still suffering with severe lower back pain. At the airport, I had to request a wheelchair to get to and from the gate. On the ship, the main thing I did was eat and stay in my cabin. I had my stool with me, but I just didn't feel like holding everybody up because of my condition. I came out of my cabin a couple of times to hang with them, but the pain was just too much for me. I used my cousins and sister as a crutch, but after a few steps, I always had to sit down. I didn't want to stop their flow, so I stayed in my cabin. They kept checking on me to make sure I was okay, and I told them not to worry about me; I was alright. I said, "Go ahead and have a good time." I really felt bad. I wanted to party, sing karaoke, and do all the things I would normally do on a cruise, but I couldn't. I really wanted to show them a good time because that was their first cruise. I have to make it up to them one day.............

Since I suffered so badly on the 3-day Bahamas cruise, I cancelled my 7-day cruise which was in May, 2009. I paid for my cruise almost a year before I got sick. Even though I was sick, I still thought I would have been able to go on the cruise; that's why I didn't cancel it sooner. Since I cancelled after penalties began, I lost $700.00 because I didn't have vacation protection. I really didn't want to suffer anymore, so I did what I had to do. It was also too late to do a name change, so I had to accept the financial loss.

I was also invited to attend various festivities, but I didn't go because I was in too much pain and didn't want my family and friends to see me in agony.

21

Heart Palpatations

Although I was taking Prednisone for neurosarcoidosis, I had other problems that required me to be hospitalized. In May, 2009, I had gone to see my chiropractor for treatment. When I told her that I was having chest pain, and that my heart was racing, she told me to go to the emergency room. I called my pulmonary doctor, and she told me to get to the hospital as quickly as I could. When I got there, my pressure was taken, and it was elevated. My heart was also beating very fast. My doctor asked me if this had ever happened before, and I told her it did. The first time it happened, I was asleep and was awakened by it. I got out of bed, and took my pressure. It was 167/100, and my pulse was 180! I was really scared! I didn't really want to go to the emergency room, so I just sat at my kitchen table for two hours and monitored my pressure until it went back to normal. I didn't start having regular episodes until a couple of weeks later. Whenever I took a shower, my heart would start racing. Whenever I did anything that caused exertion (no matter how small), my heart would start racing.

I was placed on a heart monitor, and my doctor ordered a series of tests. There were certain tests that could only be done on inpatients, so I was admitted to the hospital for a few days. When I got up to my room, I went into the bathroom to freshen up. All of a sudden, a nurse started banging on the bathroom door. She asked me what I was doing, and I told her that I was washing up. She then told me to stop what I was doing because the heart monitor showed the rapid beating of my heart. Later on that night, a nurse rushed into my room to see what I was doing because the monitor showed my heart beating fast again. When she saw that I was lying down doing nothing, they knew something was wrong. By the time an EKG was done, my heart was beating normally again. A doctor asked me what medication I was taking, and I told him that I was taking Norvasc – 5 milligrams once a day. He prescribed another medication he wanted me to take as well. The first time I took it (can't remember the name of it), I had a sharp pain in my chest and a brief few seconds of shortness of breath. Since it passed so quickly, I didn't bother to say anything about it. The next morning when the nurse gave it to me again, I started having severe pain in my chest again, I couldn't breathe, and tears were flowing from my eyes! The nursing assistant who was taking care of the patient in the bed next to me rushed to the nursing station shouting, "Something's wrong with her! She's holding her chest, and she can't breathe!" By the time the nurses came with the EKG machine and did the test again, everything went back to normal. I told them to call that doctor and tell him I wasn't taking that medication anymore. He came to my room and said that my heart was racing already before I took the medication. I told him that I had sharp pain and shortness of breath after taking that medication the night before, and it was worst that morning. I wasn't taking it again. I said to him, "You know the old saying: Three strikes, you're out! Well, I don't want to wait to see what happens. You'd better find another drug to give me." He looked at me like I was crazy and left my room.

I was transferred to a private room and continued to be monitored. No matter what I did, my heart continued to beat fast. This time, the doctor prescribed Metoprolol. Guess what? My heart stopped racing! He discontinued the Norvasc, and I had to start taking Metoprolol 25 milligrams twice daily.

Because I have sarcoidosis, the doctor wanted to do a blood gas to check the oxygen level in my blood. A nurse practitioner wanted to do it a few days earlier too, but I refused to get it done because she didn't want to use Lidocaine to numb my wrist. I explained to him how painful it was for me each time I had the test done (9-10 times). The last time it was done, Lidocaine had to be injected in my wrist because I screamed so loud when the needle hit the artery. The pain was almost unbearable! He tried to tell me that it didn't hurt that bad. When I asked him if he had a blood gas performed on him before, and he told me no, I said to him, "You can't tell me it doesn't hurt that bad if you never had one done on you. I need Lidocaine!" I was starting to panic! He said to me, "If I give you Lidocaine, it will be harder for me to find your artery, and I will have to stick you several times before I find it." I told him, "I don't care. I won't feel it anyway." He walked out of my room, and said, "I'm doing it without it." I said to myself, "He doesn't know who he's dealing with." I immediately called the Department of Medicine to speak to the Director. His assistant said that she would page him to my phone number. When the doctor came back and said that he was doing it without the Lidocaine, my phone rang. I answered, and it was the Director. I said to him, "Hi, Dr. _____! How are you? He then apologized for not having stopped by to see me yet. Then I asked him in front of the doctor, "Can I get Lidocaine in my wrist if I have to get a blood gas done?" And he said, "Sure you can." I repeated it so that the doctor could hear it. The Director told me to take care, and I got off the phone. The doctor looked at me and said, "I know you didn't just call my boss and tell on me." I said, "No. I just asked him a question. I told you that I can't have that test done without the Lidocaine. I didn't say I was having the test done by you. I just asked him if I could get the Lidocaine if I had to get the test done. You heard me. You were right here." He said, "I can't believe you called my boss on me. Now I have to go to the pharmacy to get some Lidocaine." I said, "You shouldn't worry. It was a general question. Your name was not mentioned." He walked out of the room, and a few minutes later, he returned with the Lidocaine. He injected the medicine in my wrist. After my wrist was numb, he tried to find the artery. He poked me a couple of times and then said, "This is exactly what I'm talking about.

It's hard to find the artery when the wrist is numb." I said, "I don't care how many times you have to poke me; I don't feel a thing. Can you imagine what I'd be going through if I didn't get the injection?" He was surprised that I didn't feel anything. After a couple more pokes, he was able to get some blood from my artery.

The next day, he came to my room and told me that my blood gas came back okay, and that I would be discharged. He never found out why my heart was racing. Turns out that sarcoid patients can also have heart problems, but at least I have medicine that can keep it under control. ☺

22

On The Road To Recovery

I had follow-up doctor visits every month to see how my condition was improving. I also had been going to my chiropractor, and she had been working on my head and neck to alleviate the pain. She has worked wonders! My headaches were gone, and my medication dosage was slowly reduced. My neurologist ordered another MRI to see if there was a change. An MRI was done which revealed that the swelling on my brain was gone! When she told me that, I said, "Gone, like disappeared gone? Like no more neurosarcoidosis?" And she said yes. I started singing and dancing in her office! ☺ I was so excited because I didn't have to take Prednisone anymore. I couldn't stop taking it right away though. It had to be tapered down before I could stop. I was so elated! It had only been a few months since I was diagnosed, and the doctors couldn't believe how quickly my condition improved! I meditated every day. I believed by faith that I was healed! I didn't accept anything else. It's the power of will.

After I stopped taking Prednisone, I had to see my doctor and get my blood drawn. I told her that I ate a turkey bacon and eggs on an everything bagel with mayo sandwich every day while I was on Prednisone. When my results came back, my cholesterol levels were through the roof. My doctor wanted to put me on cholesterol medication, but I said to her, "I told you I was eating eggs every day. Give me a month." Once I changed my diet, my cholesterol levels went back to normal. ☺

23

Remission

I haven't had another flare-up in three years. I continue with my daily routine: I pray, perform my daily meditation rituals, read books that empower me, listen to motivational dvds, laugh a lot, hang out with my family and friends, and just enjoy living my life. It's a beautiful feeling, and I feel great!!! ☺

I've been going for my follow-up visits with my neurologist on a regular basis. I only have to see my pulmonary doctor on an as needed basis. I still have a headache every now and then. MRI hasn't shown that the disease is back, so I'm fine, PRAISE GOD!!!

I try to eat healthy and exercise on a regular basis. I also pay very close attention to my body. If and when the disease comes back, I'll deal with it. In the meantime, I'm living my life to the fullest because tomorrow is not promised. ☺

Conclusion

I look at life differently now. I don't take anything for granted, and I feel wonderful every morning when I wake up to a new day. I try to eat right and exercise regularly, and I focus on prayer, meditation, and the powers of positive thinking. I honestly believe that's what keeps me going strong! ☺

Life in itself is a blessing, and I'm grateful and appreciative to GOD for blessing me to have such wonderful, caring people in my life who have been there for me to help me cope with this disease. I am and have always been a very high-spirited, upbeat, positive individual, and I refuse to allow myself to get depressed anymore when I have a recurrence. I'll just deal with it. I stay in happy spirits, keep on smiling, and I look at it like this: *and this too shall pass.*

GOD BLESS YOU ALL!

Peace, Blessings, and Love,
Adrienne

CPSIA information can be obtained at www.ICGtesting.com
Printed in the USA
LVOW131418280313

326517LV00001B/32/P